Yell Hound Blues

poems by

Anne Barngrover

Up On Big Rock Poetry Series

SHIPWRECKT BOOKS PUBLISHING COMPANY

Lanesboro

IN®
DIE

Cover photo by Anne Barngrover
Cover design by Shipwreckt Books

Contents

Poems from YELL HOUND BLUES have appeared in the following publications:

Anti-: "*Mmmm* My Trashy Love"
Apalachee Review: "I'd Rather" (previously titled "Dumb Bitch Her") & "Tracked My Scent" (previously titled "Not Every Party")
Barn Owl Review: "Even When I was His Woman I was Still the Other One"
Caper Literary Review: "Canopy Road Blues"
The Country Dog Review: "Yell Hound Blues" (Nominated for Pushcart Prize)
Crab Creek Review: "Driving up to Georgia the Morning that I Leave You"
Contrary: "Porch-Drinking Under the Light of the Super-Moon," "Thing of Bone" (Featured Poet Summer 2012)
The Florida Review: "Morning After, Scorned"
Full of Crow: "Meteor Shower"
Gulf Coast: "Evening Prayer"
Hayden's Ferry Review: "Dear Girl or North of Frenchtown & Three Hours till Dawn" (previously titled "North of Frenchtown & Three Hours till Dawn")
Indiana Review: "This Pleasure is Only Female or Seven Hours in Apalachicola" (previously titled "Seven Hours in Apalachicola")
iO: A Journal of New American Poetry: "Away from Here"
The Journal: "Night Call"
Juked: "The Closest I Have Been to Peaceful or Stopping for Breakfast in Slidell" (previously titled "Stopping for Breakfast in Slidell")
Meridian: "All Hallows in the Field"
Michigan Quarterly: "Memory, 1999"
Mixed Fruit: "I Overripe You So" (previously titled "The Closest I Mean to I Lust You"), "What Lasts" (Nominated for Pushcart Prize)
Nimrod: "The House on the Street with a Name that Means Oak Trees"
Ninth Letter: "Bluetick Coonhound Blues" (previously titled "Bluetick Hound")
PANK: "My Shape Alone is Sin or His Color is Not Green is Not Gold" (previously titled "Your Color is Not Green is Not Gold") & Gulf Coast Blues IV (previously titled "Discovering Phosphorescent Algae Six Months after You'd Gone")
RHINO Poetry: "Thing of Beauty"
Smartish Pace: "This Poem is a Real Bitch" (Finalist for J. Erskine Poetry Prize, nominated for Pushcart Prize)
Southern Indiana Review: "When the Ghost Gives up It's Still There"
Tar River Poetry: "Finally Turning Over"
Witness: "Driving down from Georgia and the Doors are Painted Blue"

For my parents and for Kristy

WHAT LASTS

This party is a Southern spring.
It ends without warning: bottles

fish-mouthed & so darkly gathered,
someone bourbon-drunk to hollering,

the hell has gone the moon? On wetter
days, dogwoods' hoary blooms blip

behind phone wires. I teach how
words dismay: the difference of *affect*

& *effect*, of mud prints dashed on tile,
poison ivy caked in fur. Even a book

of grammar confuses *considerate*
& *considered*. Let's look & then let's

listen: a man once left me in a field
of burning cotton. He left me

on the train tracks built from moss
& sand, the place where whiskey shrinks

to cornmeal, & the moon hides
her face against a wall, where healing

becomes a howl. An ancient thing,
even now my bird of panic flutters

on nights I'm left alone. Teach me
to believe when you say this fear

won't last. I wish to learn I could
be certain: there's any difference

between *loose* & *lose*, between a stray
& just a dog who trots with garbage

bones along a gravel road. If there's
any truth in breaking down the body

parts in bed, in how you tell me
those who hurt us never last but those

who love us will. Help me learn
the difference between *being* & what

has *been.* What I know is that the dog
had worn a broken chain. What I know

waits in the distance while we sleep:
faithful sounds of passing trains.

Mouthful of Gimme

Driving up to Georgia the Morning that I Leave You

The devil scratches himself, leaning on a watermelon truck. The devil clips
wet pecans with his tongue. The devil leers from clapboard porches

& flabby asses of milk cows. I smell old coffee, hear mosquitoes
screaming in the onion grass, & I remember the night

you pushed my shoulders into the mattress, your hair dark with sweat,
slid your belly hot over my belly, gin deep on your breath, mouth

brown as a bar & said *If you loved Jesus more I would have married you.*
The devil went to crossroads, red road, dirt road, drove through

a game of basketball, long muscles shuddering like stalks of hard corn.
The devil is a monkey hooting on a fencepost. The monkey

is a sick horse with blabbed-out oysters for eyes. You'll ride her
beat-down train tracks, spurs in her ribs, howling out the name

of your known God. The devil baptizes my hips in reddest clay.
Vegetable lamb, slut of the cotton field, I am waiting to get rocked

I Overripe You So

I want you purple potatoes. I want you
fingerlings, five strong! I want you rainbow
carrot bits. I want you pink-eyed
peas. When I say *you* I mean you there: sweet
pickles in the bathtub jars. Parlay of golden peaches.
Mayhaw pepper jam. I want you
pecan oil. I want you raw
honey dense in drums. I want you risen
loaves. Orange nut want & sour cream
want & almond lemon poppy seed, I want.
When I say *want* I mean whole cloves
of want, I mean thickest slices of want,
the lickfuls & the lickfuls
& the wet spot. I want you muskmelon.
I want you pod & pole. Whenever you come
around the air meringues & moonshines.
The dirt slurs like pudding where we seed & flower.

Morning After, Scorned

A hummingbird sucks off
a bright azalea. Green lizards burst

to sparklers on my stoop.

Mudcat vibrates between
house root & dirt seed.

What do I now carry? Fireworks

still sound like someone's
knocking. When I leave, squirrels

will corkscrew inside my engine.

They gnaw through wires, & so
I'm stranded. Thinking on you

fills my mouth with leech lime.

I should know better
than to loiter. The way of it is all

perennial: You weed me out

of pleasure. You leave me & you
leave to where I cannot go,

where tires paint slap marks

& you're a kite, you're swallow-
tailed. Come back. You're

our most beautiful bird of prey.

Here, cicadas fatten & shudder
from tree sap concubines. I peel

their bodies with my spoon.

DAY IN APRIL: STONES

The time of year when sparrows chase the hawks
like black fans opening in cheeky twirls & trout's tossed up
from a water spout, battered good in Michelob.
Breakfast is the cheaper fare: Kraft singles drool
through lumps of grits in a cracked bowl. A wink
of carcass as a butterfly in blue & green.
Kudzu spangles both the tulip & the sycamore. I throw
my stones at you, the one who's always sorry.
The stones are poems. One day I'll be a bride
who's drinking beer. These poems are gift-wrapped
in something a dog will nose up on the road.

THE HOUSE ON THE STREET WITH A NAME THAT MEANS OAK TREES

When I'm at Food Truck Thursday,
someone tells me you'll be moving soon.
                    I hear the guy in Cuzzy's
Key West Shack yell out *Mama Shirley's*
            Shrimp Pocket! but I'm not hungry
                    anymore, not even
            for those Conch Fritters, since that's all

            it takes for me to drift back to that street
with a Spanish name: our parking in the dirt
                    beneath the palm trees always
hanging low, to pushing through the pink azaleas,
            all floppy & buggy from a heartbeat
                    April storm; & now I'm back
            to hauling in your red keyboard & a bag

            of deep-fried oysters after your band's gig;
back to cooking dirty rice & folding boxers
                    on the stove; to breaking
mugs & towel-dancing on linoleum; to banging
            in dead-drunk; to waking to the landlady
                    snapping branches from the orange
            tree; waking to that old hound baying

            for something that he thought was in
the trees; to you saying *dawg* then rolling back
                    into our spoons; you pulling me
back by my purse strap, every time I turned
            to leave; & I am back to Honey
                    Butter Chicken Biscuits; dead
            guppies slivered in the tank's filter;

            to the feral cat colony prowling
through hibiscus, curled tailless
                    on our car roofs; & I'm back
to how I'd shed my bracelets & earrings, leaving
            them all around the house;
                    how you'd find them

9

glinting in the cushions & the corners,

gather them up just the way you'd
gather me up after fighting, carry me to bed,
          & bring along a plate
just in case I felt like I still wanted to smash it,
       & again I have gone back,
           back again to the last time,
when Etta James gave voice to that

something deep down in my soul
said 'Cry girl' when I saw you and that girl
          walking around, so I threw
a sandwich right at your head. Ham & mayo
      splattered everywhere, & then you said,
          Annie, you said, *you need to control*
your emotions, & I went, *Well, you need*

      to control being an asshole, & you said,
We probably shouldn't speak for a while,
          & I said, well, then I did not say
anything at all, & here at Food Truck Thursday
      the hot grease burns up to the stars,
          everybody laughs,
      & eats their Cuban tacos, ignores

      the old-timer as he sags
across his banjo, wailing about missing
          the streets of New Orleans,
& I tell them all I have to go now,
      I have to leave, because of all
          these damn mosquitoes,
      you see: they're eating me alive.

YELL HOUND BLUES

My body keeps its blood just long enough to feel
that something there has taken hold: brown bubble furballing
with despair. Scalded in gnat bites, unwanted as kudzu,
I am a shorebird windmilling a crawfish boil. Wrong trail.
Wrong scraps. Food from the river. When you call me *territorial*,
it's really that this bar is too small. I drink lit oil, piss amber
on the parrot lilies of your yard. What have you planted
inside me now? Ataxia slimes like a swamp ghost, & I throw
a cherry bomb that turns into a cocktail. I want to set you
on fire. Here, the summer lasts all year. Last night, I drove home
in a bog's hot breath, lightning clotting purple sky. Something
ran down the road, up a fence & along. I thought it was a fox.
Then thought it was a dog. I thought that you would stay,
or that you wouldn't go. I watched the animal leap off
into the woods. Nothing will let me ever keep hold.
The ghost lifted in howls, & I kept driving on.

MEMORY, 1999

The summer after the tornado hit, my family
lived still in the Residence Inn, & we
had to get away.

We drove north to Amish country,
vacationed in a strip mall. That year,
the schedule at Farm Camp for the week read:

feed the goats, turn the garden,
slaughter chicken for the camping meal.
This was the summer when my pulse

would scatter if the wind picked up, would trip
whenever the sky clicked gray—
the Bradford pears had bombed

to rice confetti, road trash churned
to cloud, houses became dollhouses, the people,
dolls. When it rained, my sister cried,

There is a chicken alive tonight
that will be dead tomorrow, & I didn't care.
I chose then to believe:

we would only take the mean ones,
the bullies with glum yolks, their dirty
feathers a no-color between what's white

& brown. Each day we call
our dogs to us & hope that they will come.
It was high time now I learned the truth

about love's danger: it's how a home blows up
into an open mouth. It's how
a heart is slit—then seals—at its throat.

This Poem is a Real Bitch

while all your poems are nothing more than frou-frou
        cakes puffed into sonnets that *quiver* & *stroll.*
This poem takes it all real personal: once got an STD
        test after your poems, once up & shoved

your poems against a keg, because this poem is no tea party,
        is not some weak-ass villanelle. This poem *backhands,*
busts a cap, *cuts a rug*, gets booted off *eHarmony* & hustled
        out of bars. Your poems suckle Carmel Appletinis

& mope in their pastel shawls. But this poem bought the right
        pair of jeggings, slashes heels that could slice
a rib-eye. Your poems paid top dollar for a perm that blurs
        the line from poodle fluff to pubic hair. This poem has line

breaks that will speak for themselves. *Kittens! Darling! Lovies!*
        your poems coo over Bang Bang Shrimp
at the Bonefish Grill. Yours don't have this poem's bone structure.
        This poem is Amy Winehouse. All your poems

are Katy Perry. Your poems have the crazy eyes. This poem
        is just straight crazy. This poem could glower your poems
into lollipop wrappers. When your poems scowl, well,
        that's just way their faces look all the time, because

your poems blog for *Covenant Housewives*, spend *Menu Plan*
        Mondays mushing up the oatmeal for a pod of babies
& clucking *I am not enough*, *I am not enough* in matching
        aprons. Instead, this poem uses a bottle of Smirnoff

as a rolling pin. But still your poems' lit degrees outnumber
        your poems themselves, & they use them for something
really big & really, really important, like analyzing
        why those Greek punks fell out of the sky or turned

themselves into a tree, & this poem ran away once, as well,
        from a traveling freak show; this poem was crowned
Sopchoppy's Worm-Grunting Queen. But it's ok!
        Your poems are *so above* judging others. This poem

smokes a bowl, skinny-dips in nursing home hot tubs,
       murmurs *All they will do is judge* above the jet-stream,
because you know this poem is always a real bitch,
       & this poem could be tender as a knife for you,

smash up headlamps & puzzles, leave out all the broken
       bits & pieces, could love you like a heartache,
a fire ant's pus-filled burn, hold you gentle as a night terror,
       & cackle while you squirm.

THING OF BEAUTY

Chicken skin bunched to the knob

       of a drumstick. Prepackaged

strawberry flower. Light gunned

       down in green rows: cathedral

of pecan. Anyone says *let go now*,

       but look at how the world

holds on: in the dollarweed, last

       hound bayed to night's deep.

From a bucket, last crawfish

       twitched before boil.

Without you near, I am the hard-

       faced shed with a heart

of blue rot. I am home to rat snake

       & shutter-vine. Take

your apologies to your religion.

       See what miracles you can

perform this time. Things

       that fester are built to last

it all: through a controlled

       burn, through a civil war.

WHEN THE GHOST GIVES UP IT'S STILL THERE

All that summer, my grandfather couldn't
breathe. His valves were choke coils.

His lungs were spent. The monitors
whirred with insect's love song: *I want,*

I want, & I was there. Crepe myrtle
knuckled on my window pane. I clocked

that big old pulse of a saw palm. No one
teaches you afterwards how not to see a dead

man's hands in the trees. The boy I loved
grayed my sheets the nights he visited,

& we clung on because you can drown
in your own body, & I never wanted

a body alone. I wanted his sadness,
the ways it filled me, more than water

till I was water, & he could put his hand
through me & feel the tide. Only women

left the hospital. My mother, she said,
birth & death, they are the same. It's always

hard crossing from one world into another.
But no one taught me how to ebb lower

than far, how to float when he held me
& pleaded, *Annie, Annie, let*

me go. I'm not all what you think I am.
It was the summer when I closed his eyes.

Day in April: A Girl, The Boy

When I was a girl, the boy next door threw chalk
at my dog's tail. I drew a line in the clover. A rope
swing set apart our lawns. I brought a tree home,
roots threading a Ziploc, & then he yanked it
from the ground. That spring the twister hurled
sunflower seeds to zigzag. A cardinal bloodied
in the grass. A pair of panties flagged his yard.
I'm sick of all of this: boys pinching sticks & skin.
You, the one who's always sorry: you could be
more clever. Go ahead & call it even. Seed
& bird & blood. Don't apologize. Just use it all.

Meteor Shower

For a moment we believe.

We rush to the back deck, grip wood
        wet-curled as soap flakes, & squint

        into the sky wedged

in the sagging fronds of a browning
        banana tree. I wear slippers knit

        by the girl before me,

your pajama pants slung at my hipbones.
        The night here is a sponge bath.

        A pumpkin softens

at our feet. We hope to see the meteors falling
        the way I once hoped for flurries

        even in warm places

ashen with mud & sleet. We peel the night's
        skin back, strip clouds like fat

        from meat, seeking the brightness,

seeking it bald. The oaks are green the soft
        of velvet; Spanish moss shimmers

        on branches & wires, on us

if we keep still. Only light the kitchen light.
        Only sound the washing machine.

        I breathe detergent & rotting

rind. I want to believe in us for longer
        than this now, want to remember you

like rain on a night that never

rained, your body earthed against sheets
    white as ropes of snowfall.

    Once we woke to owls crying

in the oak trees. Once I woke to you
    kissing me *I'm sorry*.

    For you, I break open into a thousand

streaks of light: my heart purpled,
    then opening, its bloom the wildflower

    named after the shooting star.

MMMM MY TRASHY LOVE

Hey baby, I know we're fighting again
as that Varmint-Slayer guy with a rattail
sprays roaches in the room next door. But I swear
if I don't just love & blame
every shitty little part of you, down to the mudbug
juices in your cuticles, & *aw now*
I'll lug you around in a stroller
that's filled with Vicodin & korn dogs, cuz honey,
your hair is a Burger King bikini brawl,
your skin a Natty Lite that's thrown
against the screen. You straight fool! Oh!
baby baby baby *baby*, look: your sex
drive is a pickup truck that's acid-bombed,
& I promise I won't say *I'm gonna kill you*
any more. Because we all know I'm the trouble.
I'm face-pushing those hussies
for the toilet stall when all you want's a whiskey ginger,
& those new money hipsters will never
know me like you do, cuz my eyes
are meth-heads mooning a school bus,
my middle finger a crack pipe stashed
in a cop car—but really, baby, my pride
is just a coloring book that somebody set on fire,
& my love for you is that old ringwormed floozy
who dumps your mother's ashes out a car
window, just so she can be the only one held in your heart.

CANOPY ROAD BLUES

You just need to feel it,
they all said to me, so then I let myself feel it

the only way that I knew.
Florida summer turns Florida fall

just the way colors soften when it's dusk
or after rain. From my deck the webs

of banana spiders break
like wine glasses when swept & scattered.

Beneath my window a tree frog
chorus croons a lonely serenade. This story

has a predictable ending.
This story belongs in a sinkhole.

There are only so many times
a Southern man can leave in one season,

only so many girls scallop-
dredging along the trashed gulf shore.

Their oysters glop with tar balls.
& I know I'm the hummingbird moth

while everyone yelps *hornet!*
I'm the kind that will sit tight in a hurricane.

I'll haunt egrets after I'm gone,
& I'm the cottonmouth slashing wild

blackberries, the lone ghost-
bike peddling down a darkening canopy

road until I can drape myself
in vines, shrink down to just a leaf

when it all becomes too humid,
when the constellations itch like the bites

of fire ants, pushing in far too close.
If things would just stay where

they once belonged:
cicadas in the crab grass, Spanish moss

like sorrow hanging from the wires,
his thumb pressing against the button

of my skin between hipbone & thigh.
My bed becomes a swamp of rotting gator tail.

All night long I cast off leaves
that brown, redden, & yellow well before my fall.

Even When I was His Woman
I was Still the Other One

He brought a girl to the party with thighs
        like cut wire. I whiskey-braided a short fuse.
                Her voice, my God. I remember

having just as much to prove, being caught up
        by the wrist like that, & then one day
                I woke up hiding

in the saw-grass & did not know how
        I'd gotten there: my skirt snagged
                with dull metal, my fingers whorled

with ash. Don't let him find me again, lure me
        out with saltlicks & red haw. He brought
                a book to the party to give back

to me. She must have guessed & so wanted
        it gone. If I'm a scallop, I taste
                sweaty. If I'm a panther, I'm a key

deer's shadow on a dark road. He's tricked
        the light. Wasted, I can't leap
                from his car's swerve. Don't

let him find me tonight so lonesome,
        singed & still running
                with his bullets in my hide.

THING OF BLAME

These brown sand dollars piss

      along the truck bed. Boiled

peanuts blister in their Styrofoam.

      I'm burned in finger marks,

blued where fingers cannot go.

      Someone locked that dog

in a chicken coop. Someone

      swiped the zipper peas & swan

eggs, too. Spring-heeled Jack,

      they call him. His hooves track

over roofs of barns. He follows sin

      on his hind legs to a crossroads.

You'd better pray to an appleheaded

      dog. Your ass had better be ditch-

grown. A thing cast out was once

      too much desired. Drive me

away if you feel it so. I'm still

      the red of your dirt road.

I'D RATHER

You can't trust such a baby voice, such chewed
bangs, her red mouth a smudged thumbprint
of rabbit jam, as she simpers through her flute
of Chardonnay. Watch her turn down
the crossed-legged quail. She can curry comb
but not hoofpick. She flings the onion's
yellow heart. Look over at her now:
she's lifted from the clearance rack.
She's a bullfrog squeezed into her off-season
suede & all because my love
is a dark-eyed man, because I was a fool
in the garden. In bed, his breath's a moth
so beautiful to my throat. He tells me,
You do a better job. In the pine woods
that surround us, night birds descend
like black umbrellas. Somewhere
cross-town, she dirties yet another bar.
I'd rather blame her than the belly
warm against my back. I'd rather blame
him than my heart, its vegetable drying
to dug bone. When he stirs, the dog stiffens
in her corner. When we kiss, that bitch growls.

TRACKED MY SCENT

A bottle of beer reddens, a book's pages char
       in bonfire, a black dog's tail wags too close

to flame. My feather boa molts while she scraps
       up all my dregs, then laughs a harpy's bell & points at me:

that's her. She rubs his chest in quickest curls. He'll drive
       home with her. But does she know that once there

was a party where he tracked my scent through rooms,
       where we kissed against a house so hard my earrings

broke off, & his handprint streaked my dress with mud? We'd
       hopped a wood-broke fence & walked the streets lit green

from drunken porches, necking at every oak & palm. Our knees
       had gone all rickety. Our hearts were caught shrimp flickering.

How many parties did we fool no one in the pockets & whispers
       & stalls & what all gets done behind somebody else's home?

AWAY FROM HERE

Labor Day weekend: we unraveled
the miles to our friends' trailer
for a party squeezed in sweaty
groves: to sangria in cold mason jars,

hymns tinkered on an upright
painted green, a river out of tune.
A flock of guineas perched
in gutters. From Tallahassee

to Sopchoppy, I picked the scabs
of his small talk, snapped
my bathing suit like bubble gum,
the farm road ticking off the last

exhaust of summer with its tongue.
We swam in a musk of no-see-ums.
His skin was a September
Bourbon, & his mouth was full

of poker. I lusted for him just the way
a pine tree pushes roots into blue
dirt, deep as the gully between
two stars. This summer,

it seemed as though he dredged
women from a bayou, these
women who knit hipbones
out of rain. He took their wild

bodies. He swears he imagined
each was mine. & still tonight,
the guinea fowl will leave their
roosts, make their way across

the river that has called to them
since hatchlings. At dawn, we find
the feathers, snared in rocks,
in branches, in the cur dog's mouth.

NIGHT CALL

If ever there was much difference between love & nailing
owls to your door, it has been lost on me long ago.
This logic is heat lightning. What you ward off must be
what is evil: the fat that's in my hips, headlights stripping
bones of pine needles & rat-picked fries. Lamps cool
on your glass. A horned bird's whooping in your wood.
By day, I curse you in your hollow. By gin, you'll call me
& say *wanting*, & say *wild*. I'll pour you milk scared bloody.
I'll cook brown eggs to ash. If smoke will follow beauty,
if salt will change the color of the flames, if you will walk
a circle round a tree, I'll keep turning till my neck wrings
clean. Too evil for a name, the owl is called *the bird that makes
you afraid*. Look here now: my eyes are still this green.

LOVE JESUS MORE

This field of barbeques in barrels
tried to be a churchyard just the way
he once tried to lace me down

with his lies. In the end, only one
got what he was after. Only
one of us could sing, *I got mean things*

on my mind. If even grits can suffer
then maybe the difference lies in
what we will remember: the look like

buckshot in our shop girl's eyes
the time he grabbed my wrist like a play
in football, his body taut up & over

our fried chicken. If I just learned
to keep my good trap shut. If I just
learned to love Jesus more. He moved on

the way dirt bloodies a vacant lot
into a praying ground. His new girlfriend
is a rag doll of rabbit bones. In church,

a couple tells her, *It sure is a pleasure*
to watch you two together. Sorry
for laughing: now that's just mean.

Dear Girl or North of Frenchtown
& Three Hours till Dawn

A girl's shrill scream *Hate you!* tears the night

like dried tar cracking on a snake-necked road.
    The world was not that still and now

        it proves less so. In wet grass where stray

    dogs run, Funyuns bags & cellophane wrestle

from the gold ragwort & chicken wire. An armadillo
    bolts into a bog of chemicals. Green anoles squeeze

        to brown, & through the muddy light

    of a street lamp, I see a teenage girl who spits

& writhes between her boyfriend's fatback hands.
    They live with their baby in the garage next door.

        She hollers out *I hate!* words that thrash

    like possum tails out of her tongue.

There's so much love until it all goes wrong. I too was a girl,
    once, & took the jam jars to the gutters, filled them

        with green rain & black tadpoles.

    Then one day I stepped shoeless from the porch

& onto the back of a frog ripe as a bloated strawberry,
    perfect curve to fit the arch of my small foot.

        My scream rattled the cotton from their stalks

    in our backyard. Dear girl, you must know now

how nothing ever comes out the way it should:
    the barking tree frog seems a distant

pack of hounds, the panther like the cry

of a lost child. What ghosts are these that haunt

the windows of our Southern towns? Dear girl,
     when someone says that *You're a strong woman*,

          he's only gearing up to hurt you more.

LEAVING HIM FOR GOOD THIS TIME

The oyster bar quiets,
& pints stand sudsy as sea glass.
Box fans churn rust
from their lungs like good
old boys with their menthols.

My love & I stand
in the gravel lot.
We stand & know
that soon we will grow distant
as the creeks where
the deer pause
& as the brackish waters
that coax up sea's peculiar notes.

I sit in my car while a rainbow
in gold sky blurs spilled beer
in the window's light.
Bless my heart that I mistake
black bugs for rain.
They streak against
my windshield: each break
a new knowledge I must wipe
clean before I leave.

Handful of Much Obliged

EVENING PRAYER

When you think of me, don't think of me wooing
    the bed all thick-tongued with vodka.

        Don't think of me baby-
    oiled in a green bikini with dirty feet.

Don't think of me grabbing the shrimp,
    wet and pink, from the bowl,

        seizing the whiskered face
in my fist and yanking hard. Think of my jaw.

Think of the secret I told you that scared you
    into prayer. Think of the cardboard graves

        for fake babies I kicked over
on spring break in St. Augustine.

O God, come to my assistance. O Lord, make haste to help me.

I don't want your forgiveness. Nobility bores me—
    so does shame. I watched as that girl

        in a blah cardigan called me *sieve*,
code for *slut*, code for no one ever told her

what you really thought for me. Beautiful.
    Once, so were we. Sometimes I still scan

        the night sky for a blood ring
around the moon just to feel again

that winter lying on our coats outside
    the Blues joint in a fried catfish dark:

        everyone kicking up their feet
and everyone drinking PBR and everyone

getting high in cars were merely dust spun into shapes

and we were the ones on tenterhooks.

O God, come to my assistance. O Lord, make haste to help me.

We were the ones inscribed in black
oak dirt like a vesper that would haunt

my nights for years, that would lift your new love's
skirt and murmur *envy* in her ear

as she lay sleeping in your bed.
When you think of me, let me think for you.

Remember how every time I see smoke above
the trees, I believe that my house is on fire.

ALL HALLOWS IN THE FIELD

Little spirits candle-light
      the hawthorns. Bales

of hay unroll in whipped
      rough tongues. Black horses

course the darkened pastures,
      touching nothing just

the way the night will touch,
      & birds drop from their fence

posts with the weight
      of Bibles. This is how

I waste my love on you:
      spiderwort still pinning blue

ash trays & the moon rising
      ugly as a white crooked

finger. Little spirits dash
      their teeth in the pumpkin

patch. I watch the devil take
      the corn stalks' edge.

He pours two bones
      of whiskey for the lost.

He keeps on pouring
      till the field turns brown.

DAY IN APRIL: TOO BUSY FOR SORRY

You are sorry. You are sorry. You are drunk.
Tornado razed Tuscaloosa. In Florida we host
a benefit at the bar. I cuss in burrs & safety pins. *Sir,*
I am not dumping this fine whiskey. Piss the secret
passage. Shimmy the no-cross line.
The moon gets sick in parking lots. Stars wag
their tongues in a violet grilled sky. I was
busy yelling for the dogs to come on home,
too busy throwing all my money on the ground.
The hell I was there in red shoes & black
dress. The hell I was there looking out for you.

THING OF BONE

Bloodspot knuckles into pale pink

      lace. Lips split in their corners.

How can I bargain with you when

      I want you still? Out-cry

the loud barred owls. Thumbprint

      the soft part of my thigh. I have

been to a church that was made of bones.

      Fingers spelled scripture. Skulls

lay rough-bunched behind bars.

      Things of ancient madness:

a blind monk scavenged gravesites.

      You begged scab-eyed,

naked on wet floor. Enough begets

      enough. I will baptize my daughter

in sink water on the day she is born.

      I will blow my breath into the tiniest

bones of her innermost ear,

      bones hidden even from God.

My Shape Alone is Sin
or His Color is Not Green is Not Gold

We trim later this year, my girlhood tree
        of dog-bit angels & clay stars,

wool knotted into snowmen & sheep,
        tree skirt an electric train. I'd run

its circuit as a child till sparks licked
        wheels & till the toy became

a flame. In his faith, men fast for women
        so that women may absolve.

For him, my shape alone is sin.
        A fast is just a way *to starve.*

It's what I did when he was true
        no longer—chickens drowned

in their stove pots, biscuits crumbled
        under napkins. My jeans

slimmed down to leggings. Black
        dresses unraveled to scarves.

He held me as though a bag of flour,
        ringed each ankle with his grip.

At home this holiday, women gather
        to chop dates & braid in loaves.

They brown the apples with spices,
        spell out names into the dough.

I eat from a red plate, my back to fire
        in its small brick cove. A new year

now & I must let go my resolve to love
        him till my body becomes a fast,

a prayer, a light strand set to flicker,
      no more to decorate his home.

CIGAR TREE

This smell is country, & whatever it is
I remember I remember well.
Beyond the hail-broke houses, porches
pockmarked with cans of beer,
the wood gone dark from rain
& wet sawdust of *gonna do it later*,

past dirt lots fringed with corn stalks,
the vine sprawl of white pumpkins,
past the deep red bells of barbeque,
& the banjo of chess pie: everything
has changed. Whatever woods

I ran through as a child were once
struck red & sun-cradled
like a bloodied brilliant heart,
a place I thought that only I could see.
This is the world in a splendor

of loss: every particle boot-crunched
& aching, every spitting cat & howling
dog, every flight of birds cursing
through gray sky. I know
now how the heart becomes

an owl pellet dropped dry & filled
with fur, feather, & bone: parts
of you that I still keep, no matter how
you will forget my story, no matter
how you won't think of my name.

THE CLOSEST I HAVE BEEN TO PEACEFUL OR STOPPING FOR BREAKFAST IN SLIDELL

The Vietnamese po'boys shop is closed
on Sundays, so Kent & Lauren & I
just bottom out into the gravel lot

of an off-road gumbo shack, done up
with string lights & once painted
the white of those knick-knack angels.

Today holds all that's left of our September:
the sky French blue, grass yellowing
as though with chicken fat. The air

holds sugared meat & dripping links.
Inside, straw-poke dolls grin
from windowsills, an ochre color

that'll never stain Louisiana falls.
Kids in fleur-de-lis shirts draw
on placemats while the Saints' game

buzzes low on radio. Deep-fryers
splutter, then they hum. Lauren orders
herself a little country gumbo, Kent

an egg & ham croissant, I some
sausage & French toast. Kent pays.
We three sit on the porch with two

coffees & a Barq's, & it is the closest
I have been to peaceful in so long.
I remember that you told me, when you

rid me from your life: *People fall apart.*
This happens. I am not a child. Down
the road, Kent's sisters once wrecked

their car after they got tanked at the
Daiquiris & Creams. Lauren says
that—down the road—Katrina battered

this town to not much left but gas
stations that hope to get you gone.
She tells me, it's the water that does

some of it, but mostly, it's the wind.
It's what the heart learns to stop missing:
this pushing through, that pressing clean.

GULF COAST BLUES

Of course I drown. I mean for you to see me.
The ocean is the boring apex of all sorrow, a drained-
out sump of kelp & flabby monsters. Maybe
the jelly stings in self-expression. It's less painful
than your apology. I wreck my toenail
on a sand dollar. You inspire my naming every trash barge—
U.S.S. *Little Jit. U.S.S. All You Ever Do is Fail*—
& I'm so mean I deserve this sea of weak old discharge
where I spool blood on sand & fling stale chips at gulls.
Once, when waves flicked wrists of silver & of gold
you asked me, *What should I do with you, girl?* I was so full
of rogue & love, that I just laughed & told
you *anything*, but should have said, *be careful.*
Even swimming farther, I meant to feel your pull.

***

--*National Geographic* Oct. 2012 headline: *Giant Mysterious Eyeball Found on Florida Beach*

Their hands now pull & pull, & out comes this "eyeball."
You never make sense either. I'm done using logic
to force you to want to stay. We all call
out the scientists on their cheap foul tricks:
Oh, it's fish. It's mammalian. It's from a giant squid,
& I've read they taste like ammonia. It is an old
Jawbreaker, & everyone is stupid. You simply get rid
of me after I bring you plates of food. I need to be told
twice or more. Look, it's just an ashtray. It's from a Bluefin Tuna.
Now you say, come back. Please. It's one of those nasty
rotten Chinese eggs. I know this to be true: The moon
or God must be sporting an eye patch this evening. Tell me
I am not losing what I can feel is getting tossed.
It's beautiful, whatever it is. I'm not sorry that I lost.

***

It was a swordfish that had lost it: cerulean eye cut
down to the bone. What precise savagery! What rudest form!
You are familiar with such sluttery:

44

you need me when you need me. I am lovelorn,
& you are drunk on rum. Who would do that? Hack
out a baseball-sized peeper & then just let it go?
It would go well perhaps with butter & with garlic.
If we cleaned it out, it would sure make a pretty bowl.
Head hewn off for crab bait: rash glob
of slash & spear. Cruel one, my love for you is part
& parceled. My love for you is bulbed & lobbed.
This mystery will worry us no longer. Your heart—
I know it—simply fell. Blue eyes aren't that common in the ocean.
Describe the tides: they hurt me more in slow motion.

***

How should I describe this all for you? One moonless night
in autumn we river folks swung loose a half-drunk
Maker's bottle & rushed the sea-lights
in our skivvies, our heels thumping into cold sand. You punk,
you disbeliever—half a year has gone & still I feel
you right behind me. I feel your gaze sizing me down.
The small waves lipped & pulled. We were as chilled
as whiskey offered. Here you must believe me: I found
the water lit at my fingers & at my hipbones, at shoulder blades
& ankles when I kicked & twirled. The sea was dark
but was not black. The lights were clear not made
from stars, not green not white not blue. Sparks
of phosphorescence all around me, & still you'd say *too hard*.
You've tapped out all my secrets: shells broken into shards.

***

New love of mine, here all my secrets will unfold:
I went down to the seaside. Wanted
still to be his home. Clams popped their lips like cold
fish sing the blues. Drawers of water flaunted
negligee. He said I wasn't worth
the price of a plane ticket. He said, *You never
want to be alone.* I granted him a darkened berth.
Sat down on some wet driftwood & screwed my hair
into my palms. Someone was getting married.
My dress was stained with shrimp sauce.
Sand caked between my toes. You would be wary
of the tide pools. You were years beyond my loss.
I wanted to be alone then. The sky let out its breath.
I never knew, that in the ocean, red eyes turn blue after death.

45

FINALLY TURNING OVER

Over pitchers of beer & plates of gray raw oysters,
everyone gives advice to the girl with her new
broken heart: burn the bed, the quilts, smoke

from glass green pipes, & if all else fails, just go
find somebody new. They were wrong
about this winter, too. In late January, a fog rolled

in from the swamp & with it brought the seagulls
perched on fence posts, cabbage unfurling in their
fallows, a black bear loping down the parking lot

of Taco Bell. Come February, trees punched out
their valentines: flowers hollering roadsides in pink
& red & purple. Last fall, the turkeys' breastbones

had not spotted. Onions' skins had thinned just so.
I had time to notice everything. I had time
to see nothing at all. You were coming in with the fog.

I hadn't even guessed. This winter, rain again. Birds
turn into color. Dogs turn into mud. My broken heart
becomes a lemon tree unfrozen. Oh, come to bed

with me, my dear. It's been the longest wait.
I'll flip the mattress from its bog-like garden. I'll buy
us all new blankets. You're worth unseasoned love.

BLUETICK COONHOUND BLUES

Darlene has come on home now.
We circle broken lawn chairs,

set cucumbers in the vodka

& fillet the speckled trout,
all blue-eyed & egg-bellied,

its bones like small pricked

hairs you pile in the grass.
Darlene is a Bluetick Hound.

Before us, she starved down

to a hot wire. Her leg broke
& drained campaigns.

She was taken & returned

& taken & returned. I watch
your face flushed in cheap

beer ecstasy. I watch you

pop fried bits of roe. Forgive
me if what I knew of trust

keeps hold: he yanked

my chains red-raw. He had
me run this way, baying

front porches to dirt roads.

Forgive me if I stare at you
like the dog stares

at the screened door.

Every day, she learns
to *heel & girl, no pull.*

Porch-Drinking Under the Light of the Super-Moon

June bugs sling between clay pots of apple mint
& basil, their leaves lit green in tremors
that curl around the wooden rail. A tomato plant
spurts from a Solo cup. Just beyond, a feral
cat limps onto lamp-bright sidewalk. A year ago
this night I held my grandfather's hand even
as his heart gave way, each breath rapt in halted
plastic from pump to rip to the hushed beating
of roach's wings. How do we track the pulse
of strength or fear? Which lights prove the illusion?
Which lights will gutter or flare? More than
anything I want, I can't be afraid to say *I love you*.
Fermented grape & apple in my sangria: I love you.
My friends, all chain-smoking in their flip-flops:
I love you. & you, my dear one: I know the way
you squint in the light of my dim bathroom.
I know the way you smile, your hands messed
in my hair, the brightest tick-mark of your every
scar. I love you. I love you. You lift a hand
to me, so intimate a gesture, the way you brush
an insect from my breast.

THING OF BLUES

Tree frogs swell the rainfall

      with snapping rubber bands.

Mimosas doze, blushing

      poms. Millipedes pretend

they're trains transecting ferns'

      damp slough. Such are the days

I miss the deep sadness

      I have known: dead breaths

stamped in gravel, haunting us.

      The woods will serve as my

confessional when I say I am

      not guiltless. Hardest to forgive,

this: that I reaped a thousand seasons

      for his heart. Where was it

in the pile, deer-picked & overripe?

      Fogs lift from steel tracks

after rainstorm. New love, you must

      believe: I'm letting go

another thousand times,

      a thousand ways or more.

THIS PLEASURE IS ONLY FEMALE
OR SEVEN HOURS IN APALACHICOLA

We came here for Coronas in cool cans
        & baskets brimming blue crab, grouper
                flaking in thick tongues that speak

& sweet muscles of coconut shrimp gleaming
        through white paper. This pleasure is only
                female. If the sea could chance to laugh

her dimples would be oysters, raw & grit-
        lovely & plucked from their encrusted lockets
                like the keys of tiny instruments

the color of your farm boy's eye. Synesthesia
        sobs me, journeys me like how
                the highway to the ocean wets

from smoke shanties to barnacle shacks where
        sea blisters salt sea jewelry. We follow
                the drunks on home. This is all I can desire:

a shower, coolest linens, my cheek buoyed against
        your chest in a darkened room. Old hurts rinse
                out of me in waves. How strange, that all

I needed was to know: his happiness was not
        my happiness. Finally now, I release the ghost
                nestled inside. We sleep, & it is good.

Driving down from Georgia
& the Doors are Painted Blue

The devil does my dirty work: I wish you could both know & then
forget. The devil squats at Fat Mac's BBQ. The devil suckles beer can

chicken clean to beer can bone. Here's Shot Well Road & Quail Rise Road.
The signs insist, *chicks are here, & rabbits here, & Jesus is right here,*

the churches white & poor. The funnel cloud—a forest fire, its blaze
controlled—a blue house pitched on wooden stilts, a bare-armed woman

throwing branches onto smoke. Tell me I'm at no one's mercy. If I dream
a snake, my enemy lies just behind the door. Love, I killed my snake.

His jowls, they fattened, & his hands became old catfish flapping,
while his words decayed cool marbles into dung. If I will it,

he can't harm me anymore. But you, you are an open country, a church's
bright red door. I wish you might bring my animals from hiding:

black cows wading swamps, white geese pecking at carrion, goats behind
the trees, their kids spring-born, smallest devils I will meet on my way home.

ANNE BARNGROVER

Anne's poems have appeared in such journals as *Indiana Review*, *Meridian*, *Smartish Pace*, and others. She and poet Avni Vyas are co-authors of the chapbook *Candy in Our Brains* (CutBank, 2014). Anne holds an MFA from Florida State University and is currently working on a PhD in English at University of Missouri.

NOTES:

Yell Hound, or Yeth Hound, is a black dog found originally in Devon folklore, often representing the devil, a demon, or a scorned soul.

The section titles are from the Bessie Smith song "Gulf Coast Blues."

The first line of the sonnet series "Gulf Coast Blues" is after Keetje Kuipers' "In Medias Res," published in *The Journal* Issue 36.4 Autumn 2012.

Thanks to my teachers—Scott Cairns, Gabriel Fried, James Galvin, David Kirby, Elizabeth Stuckey-French, Julianna Baggott, Erin Belieu, David Baker, Ann Townsend, Margot Singer—and especially to Aliki Barnstone, a kindred spirit, who reached out to me.

For their tough and sweet love along the way, Nancy & Scott Barngrover; Kristy Barngrover & James Clear; my long-suffering readers Rachel Inez Lane, Brandi Nicole Martin, Sally Delehant, & Candice Wuehle; my Reynolds family Jennifer Luebbers, Dan Sweatt, Matt Miller, Lauren Mallett, & Ali Stine; Melissa Range, Austin Segrest, Monica Hand, Caitlyn Smith, Alyson Thiel, Avni Vyas, Wil Oakes, Trev Newberry, Emily Alford, Lauren Fusilier, Rose Bunch, thank you. To my grandparents. And thank you to Tom Driscoll for taking a chance on me and for publishing this book.

& is about out of silence an emergent cacophony of image, of imagination & is about the poets who carry sounds one at a time like precious sparks to the hearth: words cupped in their blistering hands, their impatient breaths keeping alive light & heat & racket.

> & the sky turns dark greenish
> if it were a bottle filled
>
> with purpled wine & instead of
> horizon there is this space
>
> crammed if it is your mind
> with your thoughts if they are
> the stars

IN®
DIE